Laughter's Hidden Power

Joe R. Eagleman, PhD

CONTENTS

Joe R. Eagleman

Chapter 1: Why Laughing Matters

Laughter is often seen as a pleasant byproduct of joy, a spontaneous reaction to a joke, or simply a break in the seriousness of life. But what if laughter is more than just amusement? What if it's a hidden superpower—a force capable of healing wounds, mending relationships, diffusing tension, and even rewiring the brain? In a world that often feels heavy, divided, and overwhelmed, laughter may be one of our most underappreciated tools for survival and connection. This book explores the fascinating, transformative power of laughter—not just as entertainment, but as a life-enhancing, spirit-lifting, health-boosting force available to every human being.

From ancient rituals to modern therapy rooms, from playgrounds to boardrooms, laughter has shown up in every culture and corner of the globe. It bridges language barriers, diffuses conflict, and strengthens bonds between strangers and loved ones alike. Yet, despite its universality and its effects on the mind and body, we rarely take laughter seriously. We don't often pause to ask: Why do we laugh? What happens in our brains when we do? Can laughter help us heal? Can it improve our mental health, enhance our relationships, or even help us navigate grief? This book aims to answer those questions and reveal just how vital laughter is to living a full and resilient life.

As we journey through the biology, psychology, culture, and practical application of humor, we'll uncover how laughter improves physical health by lowering stress hormones and boosting immunity. We'll see how it supports mental health by easing anxiety and providing a buffer against depression. We'll explore how laughter functions as a powerful social glue—one that builds trust, enhances empathy, and softens life's rough edges. We'll also look at the darker sides of humor—when it excludes, mocks, or divides—and how we can approach laughter with more intention and heart.

Whether you're someone who laughs easily or someone who's forgotten what joy sounds like, *Laughter's Hidden Power* will help you rediscover the gift you already carry within you. You'll meet scientists, comedians, survivors, and everyday people who have used laughter to cope, connect, and create change. Most importantly, you'll learn how to invite more laughter into your life—not as an escape, but as a powerful way to engage more deeply with the world and with yourself. Laughter, as you'll see, is not a luxury—it's a necessity. And once you understand its hidden power, you'll never see it the same way again.

Chapter 2: The Anatomy of a Laugh

Laughter may feel like a light and effortless act, but beneath its cheerful surface lies a remarkable and complex process that engages both the body and the mind. When you laugh, it's not just your mouth and lungs that are involved—your brain lights up, your diaphragm contracts rhythmically, your facial muscles engage, and your entire physiology responds. In fact, laughter activates multiple regions of the brain, including the prefrontal cortex (associated with decision-making and social behavior), the limbic system (responsible for emotions), and the motor cortex (which controls movement). The result is a cascading event of mental and physical coordination that releases a cocktail of feel-good chemicals, such as dopamine, serotonin, and endorphins. This intricate interplay between neural circuits and body systems is what transforms a moment of humor into an all-encompassing burst of joy.

One of the key players in this process is the brain's reward center, which is the same area that responds to pleasurable stimuli like music, delicious food, and even love. When something strikes us as funny, this region is activated, reinforcing laughter as a pleasurable experience that we subconsciously seek out again and again. But laughter isn't limited to joyful reactions—it can also stem from nervousness, surprise, or relief. The brain interprets social and contextual cues almost instantly, determining whether a situation is safe enough for laughter or if it calls for a more serious response. That's why laughter can erupt during a tense conversation or in an awkward silence—it acts as a pressure release valve for the brain and body, helping us reset emotionally.

Physiologically, the act of laughing is like a mini workout. Your heart rate increases, blood vessels dilate, and oxygen intake rises—all of which contribute to a feeling of physical and mental refreshment. Just a few minutes of genuine laughter can lower levels of cortisol, the primary stress hormone, and boost immune cells that help fight disease. It's no wonder that some researchers have dubbed laughter "internal jogging." In fact, a hearty laugh can burn calories, massage internal organs, and improve blood circulation. These measurable effects point to laughter not just as a reaction but as a vital bodily function—one that contributes to overall health and vitality in ways we're only beginning to fully understand.

It's also worth noting that laughter is largely a social act. Studies have shown that people are 30 times more likely to laugh in the presence of others than when alone. This suggests that laughter evolved primarily as a bonding mechanism, rather than simply as a response to humor. When we laugh with someone, we signal trust, reduce tension, and create a shared emotional experience. Even babies as young as three months old laugh long before they can speak, showing that laughter is one of our earliest forms of communication. It requires no translation and is one of the few universal human behaviors found across all cultures and languages.

Understanding the anatomy of laughter allows us to see it not as frivolous or random, but as a powerful and purposeful force wired into our very biology. Laughter is a signal, a connector, a healer, and a motivator. It's the body's way of saying, "This moment is safe, this moment is shared, this moment is meaningful." When we begin to appreciate the complexity and design of laughter, we start to see it for what it truly is—a marvel of nature that has the power to enrich our lives from the inside out. And as we continue through this book, we'll see how this joyful act does far more than just lift our mood—it touches every aspect of our being.

Chapter 3: Early Studies of Laughter

Laughter has echoed through human history for millennia, yet serious scientific inquiry into its nature is a surprisingly recent phenomenon. In early cultures, laughter was often dismissed as trivial or relegated to the realm of entertainment and folly. However, as psychology and medical science matured in the late 19th and early 20th centuries, researchers began to recognize laughter as a rich subject worthy of study—one that offered valuable insight into human behavior, emotion, and even physical health.

The Philosophical Foundations

Before science took the reins, philosophers like Plato and Aristotle speculated on the purpose and meaning of laughter. Aristotle described laughter as a distinctly human trait and saw it as a release of excess energy. The philosopher Thomas Hobbes, centuries later, proposed that laughter arises from a sudden feeling of superiority over others—a theory that would echo through early psychological models. These musings laid a conceptual foundation, even though they lacked the empirical grounding of modern science.

Darwin's Observations

One of the first scientists to take laughter seriously was Charles Darwin. In his 1872 book, *The Expression of the Emotions in Man and Animals*, Darwin observed the similarities between human laughter and the play sounds of primates, particularly chimpanzees. He suggested that laughter was a biological response—an evolutionary trait rooted in social communication. Darwin's careful documentation of laughter's physical manifestations, such as facial expressions and vocalizations, was groundbreaking. His work helped frame laughter as a universal human behavior with great significance.

The Rise of Psychology and Freud's Influence

As psychology emerged as a formal discipline in the late 19th and early 20th centuries, so too did systematic studies of laughter. Sigmund Freud's 1905 work, *Jokes and Their Relation to the Unconscious*, was one of the earliest attempts to explore laughter through a psychoanalytic lens. Freud argued that jokes—and by extension, laughter—allow people to express hidden desires and thoughts in a socially acceptable way. He introduced the idea that humor acts as a release valve for repressed emotions, a concept that would later influence therapeutic uses of laughter.

Freud's theories were abstract and deeply rooted in his psychoanalytic framework, but they planted seeds for future exploration of the psychological functions of humor. While many of his ideas have been debated or dismissed over time, his insistence that laughter had deeper psychological meaning helped elevate the topic from light amusement to serious scientific discussion.

The Birth of Gelotology

By the mid-20th century, researchers began to carve out a specialized field dedicated to the study of laughter. This field would come to be known as *gelotology*, from the Greek word *gelos*, meaning laughter. One of the pioneers in this area was Dr. William F. Fry, a psychiatrist at Stanford University. In the 1960s, Fry conducted experiments to understand how laughter affects the body and brain. He found that laughter stimulates the cardiovascular system, increases oxygen intake, and triggers the release of endorphins—natural feel-good chemicals in the brain.

Fry coined the term "internal jogging" to describe the aerobic and therapeutic effects of laughter on the body. He also noted that laughter could reduce stress and enhance immune function. These early findings laid the groundwork for modern studies linking laughter to improved health outcomes and emotional well-being.

Norman Cousins and Laughter Therapy

Another influential figure in the early history of laughter research was Norman Cousins, a political journalist who turned to laughter as medicine. In the 1970s, Cousins was diagnosed with a debilitating spinal condition. Frustrated with conventional treatment, he began watching Marx Brothers films and reported that ten minutes of hearty laughter gave him two hours of pain-free sleep.

Cousins documented his experience in the ground-breaking book *Anatomy of an Illness*, in which he suggested that positive emotions and laughter could influence the body's healing processes. Though his claims were anecdotal, they sparked interest in the medical potential of laughter and led to more rigorous studies in the years that followed.

Laughter and Social Behavior

Early sociologists and anthropologists also took an interest in laughter, though their approach focused more on its social implications than its physiological or psychological roots. They found that laughter plays a vital role in group bonding, signaling safety, acceptance, and shared understanding. Researchers noted that people are more likely to laugh in groups than alone, and that laughter often functions as a non-verbal language of connection.

These insights revealed laughter's role not just as an individual response but as a powerful social tool. They hinted at laughter's capacity to build community, reduce tension, and foster empathy—concepts that would eventually become central to fields like social psychology and organizational behavior.

Conclusion: The Legacy of Early Research

The early pioneers of laughter research transformed a seemingly simple act into a complex and meaningful subject of scientific inquiry. From Darwin's evolutionary perspective to Freud's psychological theories, from Fry's physiological studies to Cousins' experiential insights, each contributed a piece to the puzzle of why we laugh and how it shapes our lives.

These foundational studies may not have answered all the questions about laughter, but they paved the way for a multidisciplinary exploration that continues to this day. Today's neuroscientists, psychologists, and even corporate leaders build on their legacy, proving that what once seemed trivial can, in fact, be profoundly transformative.

Chapter 4: Laughter and the Brain

Laughter might feel like a spontaneous burst of emotion, but beneath its joyful sound lies a complex and beautifully orchestrated process in the brain. When something strikes us as funny, an entire neural network springs into action—processing the information, interpreting the context, triggering emotions, and finally, coordinating the physical response. In mere seconds, the brain performs a delicate dance between cognition and emotion, thought and reflex. It's one of the most complex responses the brain can generate, and yet it happens in an instant—often without our conscious control.

At the center of this process is the **prefrontal cortex**, the brain's executive control center. This area evaluates the situation, assesses social cues, and judges the incongruity or surprise—key ingredients in humor. Much of what makes something funny depends on timing, contradiction, or an unexpected twist. The prefrontal cortex helps interpret these subtleties, filtering them through your individual experiences, beliefs, and cultural context. That's why humor is so personal—what one person finds hilarious, another may not find amusing at all.

Once the brain identifies something as humorous, it signals the **limbic system**, which governs emotion. Structures like the **amygdala** and **hippocampus** become involved, activating the emotional reaction to the perceived joke or situation. If the stimulus is strong enough, the **motor cortex** takes over to coordinate physical responses: a smile forms, your chest expands, your vocal cords vibrate, and the sound of laughter escapes. This reaction is often contagious, thanks to mirror neurons in the brain that cause us to imitate the behavior of others. That's why we often laugh when others laugh, even if we didn't hear the joke—our brains are wired to connect and mirror joy.

Laughter also triggers the release of powerful neuro-chemicals. **Dopamine**, the brain's reward chemical, floods your system, making you feel good and reinforcing the desire to repeat the experience. **Endorphins**, the body's natural painkillers, are also released, giving laughter its soothing, almost euphoric effect. Meanwhile, **serotonin** levels may rise, promoting feelings of well-being, and **cortisol**, the stress hormone, begins to drop. These biological shifts create a sense of balance and renewal, which is why a good laugh can leave you feeling physically relaxed and emotionally uplifted.

Interestingly, laughter is one of the few brain functions that involves both hemispheres of the brain. The left hemisphere processes the structure and meaning of the words, while the right hemisphere interprets tone, emotion, and context. This dual engagement shows that humor isn't just about intellect or emotion alone—it's the product of both, working in harmony. This might explain why people with brain injuries in one hemisphere often experience a diminished sense of humor, or why neurological disorders like Parkinson's or Alzheimer's can impact a person's ability to understand or express laughter.

In recent years, researchers have even begun using functional MRI (fMRI) scans to observe laughter in real-time. These studies show that laughter lights up multiple regions of the brain—more so than almost any other emotional expression. This widespread activation suggests that laughter is not a "simple" reaction, but a full-brain experience. It engages memory, attention, emotion, speech, and movement all at once. That makes laughter not only therapeutic but also neurologically stimulating. In some cases, it's even been linked to improved cognitive flexibility and mental sharpness.

When you laugh, you're doing more than reacting—you're exercising your brain. You're improving its chemistry, strengthening its connections, and deepening its capacity for empathy and understanding. In a world that often emphasizes productivity and seriousness, we overlook this vital truth: laughter is one of the brain's most powerful and beneficial experiences. It renews, it recharges, and it reconnects. And perhaps most importantly, it reminds us that behind every burst of laughter is a brain fully alive, fully present, and fully human.

Chapter 5: Healing Through Humor

The old saying "laughter is the best medicine" is more than just a comforting phrase—it's a truth backed by decades of scientific research. Laughter has measurable, positive effects on the body, especially when it comes to healing, recovery, and overall wellness. While it may not replace medical treatment, laughter can complement it in powerful ways. From boosting the immune system to reducing physical pain, humor holds healing properties that modern science is only beginning to fully understand.

One of the most profound effects of laughter is its ability to **reduce stress**. When we experience stress, our bodies release cortisol and adrenaline—hormones designed to prepare us for fight or flight. While this response can be helpful in emergencies, chronic stress leads to a cascade of health problems including high blood pressure, weakened immunity, and digestive issues. Laughter interrupts this cycle. It triggers the release of **endorphins**, the body's natural feel-good chemicals, and lowers cortisol levels. The result is a feeling of relaxation that can last for up to 45 minutes after a good laugh. Just ten to fifteen minutes of laughter a day can create real, lasting shifts in mood and physical comfort.

Laughter also **boosts the immune system** by increasing the production of antibodies and activating T-cells, which help fight infection. Dr. Lee Berk, a pioneer in laughter research, has conducted numerous studies showing that laughter increases the number and activity of natural killer cells—white blood cells that attack tumors and viruses. In this way, laughter strengthens the body's defenses and promotes resilience from the inside out. In hospitals and cancer centers, some healthcare professionals have even incorporated laughter therapy and humor programs to help improve patient outcomes and morale.

Pain relief is another unexpected but well-documented benefit of laughter. When we laugh, endorphins flood the brain, creating a natural analgesic effect. This doesn't just distract us from pain—it actually changes the brain's perception of it. In one study, participants who watched a funny movie experienced significantly higher pain tolerance afterward. Laughter relaxes the muscles and increases blood circulation, which can reduce tension and inflammation that often accompany chronic conditions like arthritis or fibromyalgia.

Beyond physical healing, laughter also supports **emotional recovery**. People dealing with grief, trauma, or depression often feel overwhelmed by negative emotions. Humor provides a way to process those feelings without being consumed by them. It offers perspective—a small but significant shift that allows us to see a difficult situation from a new angle. This shift doesn't deny the pain; rather, it gives the mind permission to breathe. Laughter becomes a light in the darkness, reminding us that joy can coexist with sorrow. That simple reminder can be enough to begin the healing process.

In mental health therapy, laughter is increasingly being recognized as a valuable therapeutic tool. Laughter yoga, for instance, blends intentional laughter with deep breathing exercises to reduce anxiety and promote emotional release. Laughter therapy groups allow participants to share in spontaneous play, often resulting in genuine, uncontrollable laughter that elevates mood and fosters community. The contagious nature of laughter makes it a natural connector, creating space for empathy and shared healing—even among strangers.

Perhaps one of the most powerful examples of laughter's healing potential comes from individuals facing life-threatening illness. Many people in cancer recovery programs or hospice care have described how humor gave them strength, purpose, and peace in the midst of suffering. Comedians like the late Bernie Siegel and others in healthcare have long advocated for the inclusion of humor in treatment plans, believing that a hopeful, joyful spirit can be as vital as medicine itself. These stories remind us that laughter doesn't only heal the body—it heals the heart.

In every laugh, there is a release. A softening. A moment of surrender to joy. And in that moment, the body and mind begin to recover, to renew, to rise. Healing through humor is not magic—it is biology, chemistry, and soul working in harmony. When we embrace laughter not as escape but as medicine, we open ourselves to one of the most profound forms of healing available: the human ability to find light, even in the darkest places.

Chapter 6: Mental Health and Humor

In a time when anxiety, depression, and emotional burnout are on the rise, the role of humor in mental health is more critical than ever. While traditional therapy, medication, and support systems remain essential, humor offers a unique and often underutilized companion in the healing process. It provides emotional distance without detachment, relief without avoidance, and hope without denial. Humor doesn't solve every mental health challenge, but it can be a lifeline—a tool for resilience, perspective, and, at times, even transformation.

Humor helps the brain navigate difficult emotions by reframing them. This is known in psychology as **cognitive reappraisal**—the ability to reinterpret a situation to change its emotional impact. When we laugh about something painful or absurd, we're not dismissing it; we're shifting our relationship with it. Humor allows us to step back from overwhelming emotions and look at them through a different lens. This perspective shift is crucial in managing anxiety, which often thrives on rigid, catastrophic thinking. A well-timed laugh can interrupt the cycle of fear and help restore a sense of control.

Research consistently shows that humor reduces symptoms of **depression and anxiety**. When we laugh, neurotransmitters like dopamine and serotonin—known as the "happy chemicals"—flood the brain. These chemicals promote feelings of contentment and ease, temporarily lifting the fog of emotional distress. Even the anticipation of laughter, such as watching a comedy or being around funny people, has been shown to elevate mood and decrease stress. Humor also lowers muscle tension, improves sleep quality, and increases psychological flexibility—all of which contribute to better mental well-being.

One of humor's greatest strengths is its ability to create **connection**. Depression often leads to isolation, and anxiety can make social interaction feel threatening. But humor builds bridges. A shared laugh breaks down walls and allows people to feel seen, accepted, and understood. Whether it's laughing at the absurdity of life with a close friend or watching a stand-up routine that reflects your own struggles, humor validates our experiences in a way that words sometimes can't. It lets us know: you're not alone.

Therapists and counselors have begun integrating humor into various forms of therapy, including **cognitive-behavioral therapy (CBT)**, **group therapy**, and even trauma-focused work. Laughter, when used skillfully, can help clients open up, reduce shame, and access difficult emotions in a more manageable way. Humor can act like a mental "pause button," offering relief and a moment of reprieve. It also encourages playfulness, curiosity, and creativity—qualities that often fade when someone is deeply struggling but are essential to healing and growth.

Importantly, humor must be authentic and sensitive to be truly helpful. Forced or dismissive jokes, especially in therapy or emotional conversations, can backfire and make someone feel unheard or minimized. But when humor arises naturally—from a shared observation, a moment of irony, or the silliness of a situation—it becomes a healing balm. It creates emotional safety, helping people feel lighter without being made to feel small.

People who incorporate humor into their coping strategies tend to demonstrate higher levels of **emotional resilience**. They're better able to bounce back from setbacks, maintain perspective during crises, and even find meaning in suffering. These individuals don't laugh to escape reality—they laugh to engage with it differently. They know that while life can be painful, confusing, and uncertain, it can also be absurd, surprising, and occasionally hilarious. This duality is not a contradiction—it's a sign of mental strength.

Humor reminds us that it's okay to feel joy, even when things are hard. It gives us permission to smile through tears, to find light in the dark, and to embrace the beautiful complexity of our emotional lives. For those walking through anxiety, depression, grief, or trauma, humor doesn't replace healing—it joins the journey. It makes the burden lighter, the road less lonely, and the heart a little more open. In the landscape of mental health, humor is not a distraction—it's a direction. A way forward, one laugh at a time.

Chapter 7: Humor as a Social Connector

Laughter is often thought of as a response to humor, but at its core, it's a deeply social behavior—a tool for connection that transcends language, culture, and age. Whether it erupts in a crowded room or bubbles up in a quiet conversation, laughter sends a clear signal: *we are safe, we are together, and we understand each other*. Humor serves as an invisible thread that binds individuals and communities, creating instant bonds and long-lasting relationships. In a world that often feels divided, humor has a rare and powerful unifying force.

From the earliest moments of life, laughter plays a social role. Babies laugh before they speak, often in response to the playful expressions or sounds of a caregiver. These early exchanges help form emotional bonds and teach the child about trust, connection, and shared joy. As we grow, laughter becomes an essential part of our social toolbox. In schoolyards, humor helps children navigate friendships, build confidence, and defuse tension. In adolescence and adulthood, it becomes a way to flirt, make friends, gain status, or signal belonging.

When people laugh together, their **brains synchronize**. Research shows that shared laughter increases the release of oxytocin—the "bonding hormone"—which strengthens feelings of trust and emotional closeness. In group settings, laughter acts like social glue, helping diverse individuals feel like part of a cohesive whole. It eases conversations, breaks down hierarchies, and creates a sense of "we-ness" that few other experiences can replicate. That's why friends who laugh together often report stronger, more satisfying relationships.

In romantic relationships, humor can act as both an icebreaker and a long-term adhesive. Couples who laugh together tend to communicate better, resolve conflicts more easily, and report higher levels of intimacy. Shared humor builds a foundation of playfulness, which allows partners to navigate challenges without losing connection. Even during disagreements, a light-hearted comment or inside joke can soften the mood and prevent escalation. Humor reminds couples not to take everything too seriously—and that love can thrive when it makes room for joy.

In the workplace, humor can transform a tense or competitive environment into one of cooperation and creativity. Teams that laugh together often perform better, communicate more openly, and experience less burnout. Leaders who use humor appropriately are perceived as more approachable and trustworthy. Humor can also help address sensitive topics, encourage honest dialogue, and boost morale. When used wisely, it fosters a culture of psychological safety where people feel valued and included.

Culturally, humor is one of the most versatile tools for bridging differences. While styles of humor may vary between regions, the essence of shared laughter—its rhythm, timing, and emotional impact—is universal. Comedy, satire, and storytelling have long been used to challenge stereotypes, critique power, and build empathy between groups. Humor can expose common ground in unexpected places, making room for conversations that might otherwise be too uncomfortable or divisive. In this way, it becomes a quiet form of diplomacy, helping us understand others by first helping us laugh together.

However, not all humor connects. Some forms—like sarcasm, ridicule, or exclusive jokes—can create distance or even harm. Humor that punches down or excludes others may feel funny in the moment, but it ultimately weakens relationships. True connective humor uplifts, invites, and includes. It's laughter that says, *"We're in this together,"* not *"I'm laughing at you."* This distinction is vital in ensuring humor builds bridges instead of walls.

In times of collective hardship—whether due to war, disaster, or crisis—shared humor often emerges as a communal balm. People gather, tell stories, and find moments of levity amid the grief. These moments aren't just distractions; they're acts of resilience. They affirm humanity, reaffirm connection, and remind us that even in sorrow, joy can still be found. Humor becomes a communal ritual that helps people carry what might otherwise be too heavy.

Ultimately, humor is not just about telling jokes or being funny. It's about recognizing the shared absurdity, surprise, and beauty of being human. It speaks the language of connection, reminding us that we are not alone. In every chuckle, every giggle, every roaring laugh shared between people, there is a message being delivered: *You matter. I see you. We belong.*

Chapter 8: Humor in Relationships

Relationships thrive on many things—communication, trust, empathy—but one of the most overlooked ingredients is humor. A shared sense of humor can be the spark that ignites attraction, the glue that holds people together, and the balm that soothes conflict. Whether in romantic partnerships, friendships, or family bonds, humor adds joy and resilience to our connections. It helps us endure challenges, deepen intimacy, and enjoy one another's company in a way that words alone often cannot.

In romantic relationships, humor often plays a foundational role from the very beginning. Many people cite a sense of humor as one of the most attractive traits in a partner. It's not just about telling jokes—it's about how someone makes you feel. Playful teasing, shared laughter, and funny observations create a sense of ease and emotional safety. These early interactions build trust and spark chemistry. A couple that can laugh together early on often finds it easier to stay connected during tougher times.

As relationships mature, humor continues to serve as a vital emotional tool. Life brings stress, disappointment, and conflict. In these moments, humor can de-escalate tension, remind partners of their bond, and provide much-needed perspective. For example, couples who face a stressful situation together—like parenting challenges, financial worries, or health issues—often find relief in joking about the chaos. These moments of lightness don't trivialize the hardship; they reaffirm the connection between partners and show that they are on the same team.

Humor also strengthens emotional intimacy. Inside jokes, funny memories, and mutual quirks form a private language that only the two people in the relationship share. This language becomes a shorthand for affection and understanding, creating a "you and me against the world" dynamic. When people laugh together, they reveal vulnerability, spontaneity, and trust—all essential ingredients for deep, lasting intimacy.

In friendships, humor serves as a bridge across differences and a mirror of shared values. Friends who laugh together tend to feel more emotionally supported and satisfied in the relationship. Laughter turns ordinary moments into memorable ones and allows people to be their authentic selves without fear of judgment. Friendships built on humor often last longer because they offer both joy and resilience—two qualities that help friends navigate the changes and challenges of life.

Within families, humor creates a sense of unity and helps manage the complex dynamics of closeness, responsibility, and individuality. Parents who use humor in a loving, non-critical way often find that it fosters stronger bonds with their children and reduces household stress. Siblings who share laughter often build lifelong connections, even if they differ in personality or lifestyle. Grandparents, too, often use humor to pass down wisdom in a way that's light-hearted but meaningful. In families, laughter becomes a ritual—a way of expressing love, remembering the past, and facing the future with courage and grace.

Of course, humor in relationships must be handled with care. Not all jokes land the same way, and humor that belittles, mocks, or controls can damage trust. What's funny to one person may feel hurtful to another. The key is sensitivity and emotional awareness. The most successful relational humor is inclusive and kind—it laughs with, not at. It builds the other person up and never crosses the line into ridicule or sarcasm that wounds.

What's remarkable is how laughter often breaks through barriers words can't. In moments of grief, silence, or even estrangement, a single shared laugh can open the door to healing. It reminds us that beneath our defenses and differences, we're still human. We still care. We can still find our way back to each other.

Ultimately, humor in relationships isn't just about fun. It's about connection. It says, *"I get you."* It says, *"We're in this together."* It says, *"No matter what happens, we'll keep laughing—and that will help us keep loving."* When nurtured and respected, humor becomes a lifelong companion in every meaningful relationship we hold.

At its core, laughter is a social signal that communicates trust and safety. When people laugh together, it signals that they are comfortable with each other and share a positive emotional experience. This shared joy creates a unique bond, reinforcing feelings of closeness and belonging. Studies show that couples who laugh together frequently tend to report higher satisfaction and resilience in their relationships.

Laughter also plays a crucial role in communication. Humor can break the ice in new relationships, ease tension during difficult conversations, and provide a gentle way to express feelings or critique without causing offense. In moments of stress or disagreement, laughter can diffuse conflict, lighten moods, and open pathways to understanding and compromise. It acts as a social lubricant, smoothing interactions and preventing misunderstandings.

Shared laughter encourages empathy and perspective-taking. When we laugh with someone, we tune into their emotional world and often see situations from their point of view. This emotional attunement fosters compassion and patience, essential ingredients for healthy relationships.

Importantly, laughter helps couples and families maintain a sense of playfulness and spontaneity. Life's responsibilities and challenges can sometimes create distance or rigidity in relationships. Humor injects fun and creativity, keeping connections vibrant and enjoyable. Playful teasing, inside jokes, and lighthearted banter become part of the unique language that defines close relationships.

In parenting, laughter strengthens the parent-child bond and supports child development. Playful interactions that include humor promote emotional security, social skills, and cognitive growth. Children learn to navigate social norms and develop resilience through humorous experiences with caregivers.

Couples and families can intentionally cultivate laughter by spending quality time together, engaging in fun activities, and embracing humor as part of everyday life. Even in challenging times, choosing to find moments of joy and laughter can transform the emotional landscape and deepen connection.

In summary, laughter is a vital relational glue that promotes connection, eases conflict, and enriches emotional intimacy. By sharing laughter, we strengthen bonds, foster empathy, and keep relationships resilient and joyful. Embracing laughter as a foundation for relationships invites greater happiness and fulfillment in our closest connections.

Chapter 9: Humor in the Workplace

The workplace is often associated with productivity, performance, and professionalism—but too often, this leaves little room for one of the most powerful tools for success and connection: humor. When used thoughtfully, humor in the workplace can transform the culture of an organization. It can reduce stress, improve communication, spark creativity, and strengthen team dynamics. Far from being a distraction, appropriate humor is a catalyst for better work, healthier relationships, and a more enjoyable environment.

Modern workplaces are high-pressure environments. Deadlines, meetings, and performance expectations can easily lead to burnout. Humor offers an antidote. A shared laugh in the break room, a lighthearted moment in a meeting, or a funny email exchange can reset the mood, ease tension, and improve morale. Laughter triggers the release of endorphins and reduces cortisol levels, helping employees feel more relaxed and energized. This emotional boost doesn't just improve individual well-being—it contributes to a positive workplace atmosphere that benefits everyone.

Leaders who use humor wisely are often perceived as more approachable, confident, and trustworthy. A manager who can laugh at themselves or lighten the mood during a tough conversation sends a signal: "I'm human, just like you." This builds psychological safety—the sense that team members can speak up, take risks, and be themselves without fear of embarrassment or punishment. When employees feel safe and valued, they're more likely to contribute ideas, ask questions, and work collaboratively.

Humor also strengthens **team cohesion**. Shared laughter creates a sense of belonging and camaraderie. It breaks down barriers between departments, titles, and backgrounds. When teams laugh together, they build trust and emotional connection. This makes collaboration smoother and conflict resolution more constructive. A funny story at the start of a meeting can encourage engagement and openness. Team-building events that incorporate humor or games often yield stronger relationships than formal workshops alone.

Creativity and problem-solving are also enhanced by humor. Laughter loosens rigid thinking and promotes mental flexibility. It encourages people to explore unconventional ideas and to see challenges from different angles. A workplace that allows for playful thinking is more likely to foster innovation. Brainstorming sessions that welcome jokes, doodles, or silly metaphors often lead to surprising and effective solutions. Humor, in this context, isn't frivolous—it's a tool for unlocking imagination and resourcefulness.

Humor also plays an important role in navigating **conflict and feedback**. Disagreements are inevitable in any workplace, but humor can be a bridge during tense moments. A well-timed, good-natured comment can diffuse hostility, open space for compromise, and remind people not to take everything personally. Similarly, constructive feedback delivered with gentle humor is often easier to receive. It softens the blow while preserving the core message.

That said, not all humor is beneficial. Misused, it can be divisive, exclusionary, or even harmful. Sarcasm, mockery, or inside jokes that alienate others create toxicity rather than trust. Humor that crosses lines— whether related to race, gender, religion, or personal boundaries—can erode respect and lead to serious consequences. The key is emotional intelligence. Humor should always be inclusive, respectful, and attuned to context. In diverse workplaces, this sensitivity is especially important.

Another dimension of workplace humor is its role in **leadership and culture-building**. Organizations known for their fun, dynamic cultures often have leaders who model and encourage humor in daily interactions. These environments tend to attract talent, retain employees longer, and earn higher satisfaction scores. Humor becomes part of the brand—not just something that happens, but something that defines the experience of working there.

In virtual and hybrid work environments, humor becomes even more essential. Without watercooler conversations or spontaneous chats, teams risk feeling disconnected. Humor in video calls, chat messages, and virtual games can reintroduce spontaneity and human connection. Even emojis and GIFs, when used appropriately, can convey warmth and personality in a digital workplace.

In the end, humor in the workplace isn't about being the class clown or the office comedian. It's about making room for joy. It's about recognizing that people work better when they feel seen, valued, and comfortable. It's about bringing our full selves to work—not just our skills, but our spirit. When laughter is welcomed, productivity rises, stress lowers, and the workplace becomes not just a place to earn a paycheck—but a place to thrive.

Chapter 10: Humor Across Cultures

Humor is a universal human experience, yet it is deeply shaped by cultural context. What makes one culture laugh might leave another puzzled or even offended. Understanding humor across cultures reveals not only the diversity of comedic expression but also the common threads that connect us as humans. In a globalized world, appreciating these differences—and similarities—is vital for communication, diplomacy, and genuine connection.

At its core, humor often relies on surprise, incongruity, and the unexpected. But what is considered surprising or incongruous varies widely. For example, slapstick physical comedy, which uses exaggerated movements and pratfalls, is often universally understood because it appeals to basic human reflexes and visual cues. However, wordplay and puns depend heavily on language nuances and often don't translate well. Jokes about politics, religion, or social norms reflect cultural values and taboos and must be approached carefully in international contexts.

Some cultures favor **direct, explicit humor**, often characterized by sarcasm or irony, while others rely on more **subtle, indirect forms** that emphasize context, timing, and social cues. For instance, British humor is famously dry and understated, often relying on wit and irony, while many East Asian cultures prefer humor that is more situational and less confrontational. Understanding these differences helps avoid miscommunication and fosters respect.

Humor also serves distinct social functions in different cultures. In some, it is a way to challenge authority, speak truth to power, or resist oppression. Political satire and social parody are powerful tools in cultures where direct criticism is risky. In others, humor reinforces social harmony by avoiding conflict and emphasizing group cohesion. Jokes might focus on shared experiences or gently poke fun at oneself rather than others. These approaches reflect broader cultural values about individualism, collectivism, respect, and face-saving.

Cross-cultural humor can be a bridge or a barrier. When done well, it fosters empathy and mutual understanding, allowing people to see the world through each other's eyes. It highlights shared human experiences like love, embarrassment, fear, and joy, reminding us that beneath cultural differences, laughter is a common language. However, humor that ignores cultural sensitivities can cause offense, perpetuate stereotypes, or deepen divides. Learning about another culture's humor requires humility, curiosity, and a willingness to listen.

Global entertainment industries demonstrate both the challenges and the power of cross-cultural humor. Hollywood comedies often try to appeal to broad audiences by using universal themes like family dynamics or workplace mishaps. International comedians who perform across borders must adapt their material, finding the balance between local flavor and global appeal. Social media platforms have accelerated this exchange, allowing jokes, memes, and viral videos to travel instantly around the world. This global sharing has created new hybrid forms of humor but also sparked debates about cultural appropriation and sensitivity.

Language plays a critical role in humor's cultural expression. Translating jokes requires more than linguistic skill—it demands cultural insight. Some phrases, idioms, or references have no direct equivalent, and humor relying on them can lose its punch. Professional translators often work closely with comedians to adapt material for different audiences, preserving the spirit of the joke even if the words change.

Despite these differences, some aspects of humor appear nearly universal. Babies and young children laugh at similar playful sounds and physical comedy worldwide. The feeling of relief that comes from laughing in the face of fear or uncertainty is a shared human experience. Humor's ability to create social bonds and ease tension transcends culture and time.

In a world growing ever more connected yet complex, humor across cultures is both a challenge and an opportunity. It invites us to be open-minded, to recognize the beauty of diversity, and to celebrate what unites us. When we laugh together across cultural lines, we participate in a timeless human tradition—one that reminds us that even in our differences, joy and connection are possible.

Chapter 11: Laughter in the Bible

Laughter may not be the first thing that comes to mind when thinking of the Bible, yet it is very much present throughout Scripture. From the spontaneous chuckles of disbelief to the joyful expressions of faith, laughter is woven into the biblical narrative as both a human and divine response. The Bible reveals that laughter is not only a gift from God but also a meaningful part of spiritual life.

One of the earliest and most iconic moments of laughter in the Bible occurs with Sarah, the wife of Abraham. When she overheard the Lord's promise that she would bear a son in her old age, Sarah laughed to herself. Her laughter, recorded in Genesis 18:12, was a mix of disbelief, surprise, and perhaps even a bit of irony. At nearly ninety years old, she couldn't imagine such a promise becoming reality. Yet God responded not with rebuke, but with a gentle question: "Is anything too hard for the Lord?" (Genesis 18:14). When Isaac was born, Sarah declared, "God has brought me laughter, and everyone who hears about this will laugh with me" (Genesis 21:6). What began as skeptical laughter became a symbol of joy and fulfilled promise. In fact, the name Isaac means "he laughs."

This story reminds us that laughter often arises when God does the unexpected. It also reveals how laughter can be transformed—from doubt into delight, from irony into awe. God didn't punish Sarah for laughing; instead, He brought her into the joy of His promise.

In the Psalms, laughter takes on another dimension. Psalm 126 paints a picture of joyful celebration as the Israelites return from captivity: "Our mouths were filled with laughter, our tongues with songs of joy" (Psalm 126:2). This is the laughter of deliverance—a deep, overwhelming joy that bubbles up when hope is restored and freedom is won. Laughter here is a communal celebration, a natural response to the goodness of God.

There are also moments in Scripture where laughter serves as a tool of contrast. In Ecclesiastes 3:4, we are reminded that there is "a time to weep and a time to laugh," placing laughter in the grand rhythm of life's seasons. The verse acknowledges that laughter is essential, but also situational—something to be honored in its right time.

Not all laughter in the Bible is positive. Proverbs warns against empty or foolish laughter. Proverbs 14:13 notes, "Even in laughter the heart may ache, and rejoicing may end in grief." This verse recognizes that not all laughter is genuine; sometimes it masks sorrow or is used as a distraction from deeper truths. The book of Ecclesiastes also critiques the pursuit of laughter as a substitute for meaning. In Ecclesiastes 2:2, the writer says, "Laughter," I said, "is madness. And what does pleasure accomplish?" These passages challenge us to consider the *quality* and *purpose* of our laughter.

Interestingly, even God is described as laughing—but His laughter often reflects divine justice. Psalm 2:4 says, "The One enthroned in heaven laughs; the Lord scoffs at them." This is not the gentle laughter of joy, but the powerful laughter of God responding to human arrogance. In these instances, divine laughter reminds us that God sees the folly of those who oppose His will, and that ultimate justice belongs to Him.

In the New Testament, Jesus is not recorded as laughing, but His teachings and parables are filled with wit, irony, and humor. He used exaggeration ("a camel going through the eye of a needle"), clever wordplay, and unexpected reversals to engage listeners and challenge their assumptions. His presence brought joy wherever He went, and people were drawn to Him not just because of His miracles, but also because of His spirit of life, compassion, and yes—perhaps laughter.

The fruit of the Spirit includes joy (Galatians 5:22), and joy often expresses itself through laughter. A faith that is alive should not be heavy and dour, but marked by celebration, wonder, and light-heartedness. Christians throughout history have embraced this truth. Many saints, writers, and thinkers have testified to the sacredness of joy and the healing power of laughter.

Laughter in the Bible reminds us that faith and joy are not separate. God created us with the capacity to laugh, and He rejoices when we use that gift in love, gratitude, and celebration. Whether it's the laughter of a long-awaited promise, the joy of a redeemed people, or the quiet chuckle of a soul at peace, biblical laughter points us toward the heart of a God who delights in His creation.

In the end, laughter is not only welcome in the spiritual life—it is vital. It is a reminder that while life is serious, it is also beautifully unpredictable, wonderfully hopeful, and often quite funny. And in that holy laughter, we find a glimpse of heaven's joy.

Chapter 12: The Science of Laughter

Laughter is a fascinating biological and psychological phenomenon that has intrigued scientists for centuries. What happens in our brains and bodies when we laugh? Why do we laugh in certain situations and not others? Understanding the science behind laughter not only deepens our appreciation of its power but also reveals why laughter is essential to our health and social life.

At the neurological level, laughter engages multiple areas of the brain. The limbic system, which controls emotions, plays a central role. When something strikes us as funny, signals from the brain's emotional centers trigger a cascade of responses. The prefrontal cortex helps us recognize humor by interpreting context and incongruity, while the motor cortex controls the physical act of laughing. The brain's reward system releases dopamine, the "feel-good" neurotransmitter, which creates the pleasurable sensation associated with laughter.

Physiologically, laughter is a complex behavior involving respiratory, facial, and vocal muscles. It begins with rapid, rhythmic exhalations accompanied by distinctive vocalizations. This physical act increases oxygen intake and stimulates the heart and lungs, often producing a mild workout effect. Studies show that laughter can improve blood flow, boost immune function, and reduce levels of stress hormones like cortisol. In essence, laughter is a natural medicine that supports both physical and mental well-being.

The science of laughter also explores its social and evolutionary functions. Humans are not the only species that laugh; many primates exhibit laughter-like vocalizations during play, suggesting laughter's deep evolutionary roots. Laughter likely evolved as a social bonding mechanism, signaling safety and shared understanding within groups. This evolutionary perspective explains why laughter often occurs in social settings and why we tend to laugh more when we are with others.

Psychologists have studied different types of laughter and humor, noting distinctions between spontaneous laughter triggered by genuine amusement and more controlled or social laughter used to communicate politeness or ease tension. Social laughter can reinforce bonds even when no overt joke is present, highlighting its role as a social signal.

Research in neuroscience and psychology also examines laughter's effects on mood and mental health. Laughter stimulates the release of endorphins, natural painkillers that promote feelings of happiness. It can reduce anxiety and depression symptoms and enhance resilience.

Therapeutic practices like laughter yoga and humor therapy leverage these effects to improve quality of life in clinical settings.

In summary, the science of laughter reveals a sophisticated interplay between brain, body, and social context. It underscores laughter's unique role as a vital, health-enhancing behavior that connects us to others and to ourselves. As we continue to uncover its mysteries, laughter remains a timeless, universal source of joy and healing.

Chapter 13: Laughter and Mental Health

Laughter is much more than just a spontaneous reaction to humor—it plays a powerful and transformative role in mental health. Across cultures and history, laughter has been recognized as a natural balm for the mind, easing emotional pain, lifting spirits, and fostering resilience in the face of life's challenges. This chapter explores the deep connection between laughter and mental well-being, highlighting scientific findings and practical insights on how laughter supports psychological health.

Mental health disorders such as anxiety, depression, and chronic stress have become increasingly common worldwide. Conventional treatments—therapy, medication, lifestyle changes—are essential, but laughter offers a complementary tool that is accessible, natural, and often underutilized. Research consistently shows that laughter reduces stress hormones like cortisol and adrenaline, lowers blood pressure, and triggers the release of feel-good chemicals such as endorphins and serotonin. These biochemical shifts help regulate mood, promote relaxation, and improve overall emotional balance.

Laughter's impact on mental health extends beyond these physiological effects. It changes our mindset and perspective. When we laugh, we momentarily step outside of worries and negative thoughts, gaining a fresh outlook on problems. Humor provides psychological distance, helping us view challenges more objectively or with lightness rather than overwhelm. This shift can foster hope, creativity, and coping.

In therapeutic settings, laughter is used as a deliberate tool. Laughter therapy and laughter yoga combine intentional laughing exercises with breathing techniques, promoting emotional release and connection. Group laughter sessions create a sense of community and belonging, which are crucial factors in mental wellness. Even simulated laughter—laughing on purpose—can trigger the brain's positive feedback loops, demonstrating that the act of laughter itself, regardless of genuine humor, has healing benefits.

Socially, laughter strengthens relationships and reduces feelings of isolation—common contributors to poor mental health. Shared laughter builds bonds and trust, making it easier to express vulnerabilities and seek support. For those struggling with loneliness or trauma, laughter can be a gentle bridge back to connection and joy.

Importantly, laughter also helps build emotional resilience. Life inevitably brings setbacks, disappointments, and pain, but humor offers a psychological shield. People who can find humor even in difficult situations tend to recover more quickly from adversity and maintain better mental health over time. This resilience doesn't deny suffering but acknowledges it while nurturing hope and strength.

Of course, laughter is not a cure-all and must be balanced with empathy and seriousness when appropriate. Forced or inappropriate laughter can feel alienating. Mental health professionals emphasize that laughter works best when it respects an individual's feelings and is part of a holistic approach to well-being.

In conclusion, laughter is a potent, natural ally in mental health. It helps regulate emotions, reduce stress, enhance social connection, and foster resilience. By inviting more laughter into our lives—not as an escape but as a tool—we can nurture our minds, deepen our healing, and enrich our journey toward emotional wellness.

Chapter 14: Laughter and Physical Health

Laughter is often called "the best medicine," and science increasingly confirms that this saying is more than just a metaphor. Beyond lifting our spirits and strengthening social bonds, laughter has tangible, measurable benefits for our physical health. This chapter explores how laughter impacts the body, from boosting the immune system to protecting the heart, and why incorporating laughter into daily life is a simple yet powerful way to enhance overall well-being.

When we laugh, our body undergoes a series of physiological changes that promote health. One of the most immediate effects is on the cardiovascular system. Laughter triggers a short burst of aerobic exercise for the heart and lungs by increasing heart rate and oxygen intake. This process improves blood circulation and helps dilate blood vessels, much like moderate physical exercise does. Improved circulation helps lower blood pressure and reduces the risk of cardiovascular disease, one of the leading causes of death worldwide.

Laughter also strengthens the immune system. Research has shown that people who laugh frequently have higher levels of infection-fighting antibodies and immune cells such as T-cells. These components of the immune system are critical in protecting the body against illnesses ranging from the common cold to more serious infections. The stress-reducing effects of laughter contribute here, since chronic stress weakens immune function and makes the body more vulnerable to disease.

Another key benefit of laughter is its ability to relieve pain. Laughter stimulates the release of endorphins, natural opioids produced by the brain that reduce pain perception and create feelings of pleasure and euphoria. This natural pain relief mechanism can be particularly helpful for chronic conditions such as arthritis or fibromyalgia. Some studies suggest that laughter therapy can complement traditional pain management techniques and improve quality of life for patients.

Laughter also promotes respiratory health. The deep breathing associated with hearty laughter helps increase lung capacity and clear the respiratory tract. For people with asthma or chronic bronchitis, laughter can improve breathing efficiency and reduce symptoms. Moreover, the rhythmic pattern of laughing relaxes the muscles in the face and chest, releasing tension and promoting relaxation throughout the body.

Beyond these physiological effects, laughter encourages healthy habits indirectly by motivating people to be more active and socially engaged. Those who laugh more tend to experience less stress and depression, which are major risk factors for physical illness. Positive emotional states also support better sleep, appetite, and energy levels, creating a virtuous cycle of health.

Despite all these benefits, laughter is often under-appreciated as a health tool because it requires no prescription, costs nothing, and feels too effortless to be taken seriously. Yet the evidence is clear: regular laughter contributes to longevity, resilience against illness, and improved quality of life.

Incorporating laughter into daily routines doesn't mean you must always be joking or comedic. Simple activities like watching a funny movie, spending time with playful friends or pets, or practicing laughter yoga can stimulate these health benefits. The key is to embrace joy and lightness as essential components of a healthy lifestyle.

In summary, laughter is a powerful, natural medicine for the body. Its ability to boost heart health, enhance immunity, relieve pain, and promote relaxation makes it a vital—and enjoyable—path to physical well-being. As science continues to uncover laughter's healing powers, it invites us to laugh more freely and often as a meaningful act of self-care.

Chapter 15: Laughter and Aging

Aging is an inevitable part of life, often accompanied by challenges such as declining physical health, loss of loved ones, and increased social isolation. Yet laughter remains a timeless companion, offering unique benefits that can ease the aging process and enhance quality of life in the golden years. This chapter explores how laughter influences aging, promoting not only longevity but also vitality, connection, and emotional resilience among older adults.

Physiologically, laughter supports many aspects of healthy aging. Regular laughter helps maintain cardiovascular health, improves lung function, and reduces stress—factors that are especially important as the body becomes more vulnerable with age. Research shows that seniors who engage in laughter have better immune responses and experience fewer illnesses. The natural pain relief provided by endorphins released during laughter can also reduce the reliance on medications, which often carry side effects in older populations.

Mental health is a major concern as people age, with risks of depression, anxiety, and cognitive decline increasing. Laughter combats these issues by stimulating brain regions involved in mood regulation and cognitive function. It encourages mental flexibility, creativity, and social engagement—key elements for maintaining sharpness and emotional well-being. Group laughter activities, such as laughter yoga or social clubs centered on humor, have shown promising results in improving mood and cognitive performance in elderly participants.

Social isolation and loneliness are common challenges in later life, often leading to poor health outcomes. Laughter is a powerful social glue that can break down barriers, foster connections, and create a sense of belonging. Shared laughter strengthens friendships, bridges generational gaps, and encourages participation in community activities. For older adults living alone or in care facilities, laughter can provide moments of joy that counterbalance feelings of solitude and loss.

Laughter also nurtures emotional resilience, helping seniors cope with grief, illness, and the uncertainties of aging. Humor provides a psychological distance from hardships, allowing older adults to reframe difficulties with lightness and hope. This perspective shift supports acceptance, reduces anxiety, and fosters a positive outlook on life's later stages.

Importantly, laughter helps combat ageism—the negative stereotypes and discrimination often faced by older adults. By embracing humor, seniors reclaim their vitality and agency, challenging societal notions that aging is solely about decline. Humor allows older adults to celebrate their experiences, wisdom, and unique perspectives with joy and pride.

Practically, incorporating laughter into daily routines is both accessible and enjoyable for older adults. Activities such as watching comedies, sharing funny stories, participating in humor workshops, or simply spending time with playful grandchildren can invite laughter regularly. Caregivers and communities that encourage laughter foster healthier, happier environments for aging populations.

In conclusion, laughter is a potent ally in the aging process. It promotes physical health, mental sharpness, social connection, and emotional strength—ingredients essential for a fulfilling and graceful journey through later life. By cherishing laughter, older adults and those around them can transform aging into a vibrant, joyful chapter rather than one defined by loss or limitation.

Chapter 16: Laughter in Education

Laughter has a remarkable place in the realm of education, serving as a catalyst for learning, creativity, and social connection. Far from being a distraction, humor and laughter create an environment where students feel safe, engaged, and motivated to explore new ideas. This chapter delves into the role of laughter in educational settings, examining how teachers, students, and institutions can harness its power to enhance teaching effectiveness and promote lifelong learning.

One of the primary benefits of laughter in education is its ability to reduce stress and anxiety. Many students face pressure from exams, social dynamics, and high expectations, which can hinder their ability to absorb and retain information. Humor breaks down these barriers by creating a relaxed atmosphere where students feel comfortable taking intellectual risks and making mistakes—both essential for deep learning.

Neuroscientific research supports this: laughter activates brain regions involved in attention and memory, helping students focus and encode new material more effectively. When a lesson is infused with humor, the positive emotional experience strengthens neural connections, making recall easier and more enjoyable. This is why educational programs that incorporate playful activities, funny anecdotes, or humorous visuals often see higher engagement and retention rates.

Beyond cognitive benefits, laughter fosters social bonds among students and between teachers and students. Shared laughter builds trust and rapport, creating a collaborative classroom culture where diverse ideas are welcomed. Humor can also break down social hierarchies, empowering shy or marginalized students to participate more fully. When students laugh together, they develop empathy and communication skills that extend beyond academic content into real-world interactions.

Teachers play a pivotal role in integrating laughter effectively. Successful use of humor requires sensitivity and awareness of cultural, developmental, and individual differences. What one student finds hilarious, another might find confusing or even offensive. Skilled educators balance humor with respect, using it to support lessons rather than detract from them. They also model how humor can be used constructively—to challenge ideas, spark curiosity, or cope with setbacks—rather than as a tool for ridicule or exclusion.

Incorporating laughter into curriculum design opens creative possibilities. Educational games, storytelling, role-playing, and improvisation encourage active participation and make complex subjects more accessible. Subjects often perceived as dry or difficult—like math, science, or history—can come alive through humor, connecting concepts to students' experiences and interests.

Laughter's role in education extends beyond formal classrooms. Early childhood educators use playful interactions to stimulate language and social skills, while adult learning programs incorporate humor to ease transitions and build community. In online learning environments, where physical presence is absent, well-timed humor and lighthearted engagement help maintain attention and reduce isolation.

The benefits of laughter in education ripple outward, influencing long-term attitudes toward learning. Students who associate education with joy and connection are more likely to pursue lifelong learning and adapt to new challenges. They develop resilience, creativity, and a growth mindset—qualities essential in an ever-changing world.

In summary, laughter is a powerful educational tool that enhances cognitive function, emotional well-being, and social cohesion. When thoughtfully integrated, humor transforms classrooms into vibrant spaces of discovery and connection. Embracing laughter in education is an investment in more effective teaching, happier learners, and a brighter future.

Chapter 17: Use of Laughter in Television

Laughter has been an integral part of television since its earliest days, serving not only as a source of entertainment but also as a tool for connection, commentary, and cultural reflection. From the infectious giggles of sitcom characters to the carefully timed laugh tracks, television has long relied on laughter to engage audiences and shape viewing experiences.

Laughter as a Cue and Connection

In the golden age of television, producers quickly realized that laughter could be used as a social cue. Live studio audiences provided real-time reactions, allowing at-home viewers to feel part of a shared experience. When characters laughed, audiences laughed along. When laugh tracks were introduced, they served as psychological prompts, signaling to viewers when something was meant to be funny. Though artificial, these cues created a sense of communal watching—even in solitude.

Television comedies like *I Love Lucy*, *The Dick Van Dyke Show*, and *All in the Family* blended physical comedy with sharp dialogue, and the laughter heard onscreen reinforced the idea that humor was a unifying experience. These shows weren't just about making people laugh—they were about building a rhythm, a structure, a shared emotional tone that brought viewers together.

The Rise of the Laugh Track

The laugh track, or canned laughter, became a hallmark of many sitcoms from the 1950s through the 1990s. It was designed to simulate the live audience experience and maintain comedic timing. Shows like *The Brady Bunch*, *Gilligan's Island*, and *Three's Company* used laugh tracks extensively, creating a predictable beat that helped audiences follow the humor.

However, critics have long debated the authenticity of laugh tracks. Some see them as manipulative or artificial, while others argue they enhance enjoyment by giving viewers permission to laugh. Interestingly, psychological studies suggest that people are more likely to laugh at something if they hear others laughing—whether real or recorded. This speaks to the contagious nature of laughter and its role in social bonding, even though a screen.

Sitcoms and the Structure of Humor

The sitcom format itself is a playground for laughter. With its compact storytelling, recurring characters, and predictable structure, sitcoms prime audiences for humor. Shows like *Friends*, *The Big Bang Theory*, and *Seinfeld* use situational irony, character quirks, and misunderstandings to deliver consistent laughs. The familiarity of characters allows viewers to anticipate reactions and find humor in the known, deepening the emotional impact of each laugh.

More modern comedies, such as *The Office* and *Parks and Recreation*, moved away from laugh tracks, instead using awkward silences, mockumentary styles, and subtle, often dry humor. These shows trusted viewers to find the humor on their own, signaling a shift in comedic taste and audience sophistication.

Laughter as Commentary

Television has also used laughter to address serious issues through satire and parody. Programs like *Saturday Night Live*, *The Daily Show*, and *Last Week Tonight* use comedy to critique politics, culture, and current events. Laughter in these contexts is not just about amusement— it's about awareness. These shows provoke thought through humor, offering catharsis in the face of complex or troubling realities.

Sketch comedy and stand-up specials on TV have served as powerful platforms for marginalized voices, using laughter to challenge stereotypes, explore identity, and highlight social injustices. Comedians like Richard Pryor, Ellen DeGeneres, Dave Chappelle, and Ali Wong have all used television to craft humorous yet poignant narratives that resonate deeply with audiences.

Emotional Relief and Escapism

Perhaps most importantly, laughter on television offers escape. In times of stress, uncertainty, or sadness, people often turn to comedy for relief. Rewatching favorite sitcoms or comedic episodes can evoke a comforting nostalgia and provide a safe space for emotional release.

During global events such as economic downturns or the COVID-19 pandemic, streaming platforms reported spikes in viewership of classic comedies. This surge underscored how deeply laughter is tied to human resilience—and how television, even in its simplest form, can be a source of healing.

Conclusion

Laughter in television is more than entertainment—it's a social glue, a cultural mirror, and a psychological balm. Whether delivered through a laugh track, a clever script, or a spontaneous joke, television laughter connects us across time and space. It teaches, heals, and unites. In the ever-evolving landscape of screen media, one thing remains clear: where there is laughter, there is life—and television continues to be one of its most powerful amplifiers.

Chapter 18: Finding Your Funny Bone

Discovering your unique sense of humor—your "funny bone"—is a personal and joyful journey that unlocks the power of laughter in your life. This chapter guides you through understanding, exploring, and embracing what makes you laugh, helping you cultivate authentic humor that enriches your relationships, boosts your well-being, and brings more lightness to everyday moments.

Everyone's funny bone is different. Humor is deeply personal and shaped by personality, culture, experiences, and even mood. What makes one person roar with laughter might leave another puzzled or indifferent. Finding your funny bone means tuning into what genuinely amuses you, rather than what you think you "should" find funny. This authenticity allows laughter to flow naturally and connects you to your true self.

Start by reflecting on the types of humor that resonate most with you. Do you enjoy witty wordplay, silly slapstick, dry sarcasm, or heartfelt comedy? Perhaps you laugh at absurd situations or find humor in everyday awkward moments. Pay attention to what sparks spontaneous laughter—whether it's a particular comedian, a favorite TV show, a playful friend, or even your own quirks.

Experimentation is key. Expose yourself to a variety of comedic styles and settings. Attend improv shows, watch different genres of comedy, read humorous books, or listen to funny podcasts. Notice how each experience makes you feel. Over time, you'll discover patterns that highlight what tickles your funny bone the most.

Another important step is to embrace vulnerability. Humor often arises from the unexpected, the imperfect, and the human. Don't be afraid to laugh at yourself or share your humorous side with others. Letting go of self-judgment invites genuine laughter and deepens connections. Remember, even the most confident comedians started by embracing their quirks and imperfections.

Pay attention to the company you keep. Surround yourself with people who encourage laughter and share your humor style. Engaging with like-minded friends or communities can amplify your laughter frequency and help you refine your comedic voice. Positive social feedback reinforces your confidence and enjoyment in humor.

Finding your funny bone also means recognizing moments for humor in daily life. Cultivate curiosity about the world's absurdities, ironies, and surprises.

Develop the habit of looking for humor in challenges or setbacks—this playful perspective nurtures resilience and joy.

Finally, allow your funny bone to grow. Like any skill, humor develops with practice. Try telling jokes, sharing funny stories, or experimenting with playful banter. Notice how your laughter invites others to laugh too, creating a ripple effect of joy.

In conclusion, finding your funny bone is a liberating and empowering process. By embracing your unique humor style and inviting laughter into your life authentically, you open the door to deeper connection, better health, and greater happiness. Your funny bone is your personal key to unlocking laughter's hidden power—cherish it, nurture it, and let it shine.

Chapter 19: Laughing at Yourself

One of the most liberating and healing forms of laughter is the ability to laugh at yourself. This kind of humor—the playful, kind-hearted acknowledgment of your own quirks, mistakes, and imperfections—not only lightens your emotional load but also builds resilience, humility, and stronger connections with others. This chapter explores why laughing at yourself is so powerful and how you can cultivate this skill with grace and warmth.

Laughing at yourself is a sign of emotional intelligence and self-acceptance. It shows you don't take yourself too seriously and can view your flaws and mishaps with compassion rather than harsh judgment. This attitude reduces stress, as it frees you from the pressure of perfectionism and the fear of embarrassment. When you embrace your humanity with humor, you open a space for growth and joy.

Humor directed at yourself helps put life's challenges in perspective. Everyone stumbles, makes awkward mistakes, or finds themselves in embarrassing situations. Instead of dwelling on shame or frustration, turning these moments into lighthearted stories or jokes diffuses tension and restores balance. It's a way of saying, "Yes, I'm human—and that's okay." This mindset promotes resilience by transforming setbacks into opportunities for laughter and learning.

Laughing at yourself also improves social bonds. When you share your funny missteps or poke gentle fun at your own habits, others feel more comfortable and connected. It invites empathy and signals humility, making relationships more authentic and less competitive. People often appreciate those who can laugh at themselves because it makes them relatable and trustworthy.

Developing this skill requires vulnerability and practice. Start small by noticing your reactions when things don't go as planned. Instead of frustration or embarrassment, try to see the humor in the situation. Share a funny anecdote about a recent blunder with a friend or write it down to lighten the experience. Over time, this playful self-reflection becomes a natural habit.

It's important to distinguish laughing at yourself from self-deprecation that harms self-esteem. The goal is to celebrate your humanity with kindness, not to reinforce negative beliefs or shame. Self-laughter should be gentle and affirming, not cruel or dismissive. Practicing self-compassion alongside humor ensures that laughter uplifts rather than undermines.

Another helpful approach is to reframe mistakes or awkward moments as "laughing lessons." Each misstep becomes a story that entertains, teaches, and connects rather than wounds. This perspective fosters curiosity and openness rather than defensiveness or denial.

In professional or social settings, laughing at yourself can ease tension and humanize you as a leader or peer. It shows confidence and approachability, encouraging others to be authentic as well. Humor can bridge divides and create a positive, inclusive atmosphere.

In conclusion, laughing at yourself is a powerful tool for emotional resilience, self-acceptance, and deeper relationships. By embracing your imperfections with humor and kindness, you free yourself from the burden of perfection and invite joy into your life. Cultivating this joyful self-awareness enriches your experience and strengthens your connection with others, revealing laughter's hidden power within.

Chapter 20: Humor as a Daily Habit

Humor is not just a spontaneous burst of laughter; it can be a cultivated daily habit that enriches your life, strengthens your relationships, and enhances your overall well-being. This chapter explores how integrating humor intentionally into your everyday routine can transform mundane moments into opportunities for joy, resilience, and connection.

Building humor into your daily life begins with awareness. It means actively looking for funny, lighthearted, or absurd moments throughout your day, whether in conversations, work situations, or even your own thoughts. Developing this habit requires training your mind to shift perspective and notice humor where you might have overlooked it before. By tuning in to life's comedic side, you invite more frequent laughter and joy.

One simple way to nurture humor daily is by creating routines around it. For example, start your morning with a funny podcast or a comic strip that sets a playful tone for the day. During breaks at work or home, watch a short humorous video or share a joke with a colleague or family member. Establishing these small rituals primes your brain to anticipate and enjoy humor regularly.

Incorporating humor into conversations is another effective practice. Light teasing, witty remarks, or playful banter can make interactions more engaging and enjoyable. Humor fosters rapport and eases tensions, especially in stressful situations. It's a tool for creating positive social connections and building emotional safety.

Journaling can also be a powerful way to cultivate humor. Keeping a "humor journal" where you jot down amusing incidents, jokes you've heard, or funny observations helps reinforce your attention to humor in daily life. Reflecting on these moments boosts mood and provides a reservoir of laughter you can revisit during tough times.

Practicing mindfulness combined with humor can deepen this habit. When you notice tension, frustration, or negative thoughts, pause and try to reframe the situation with a humorous angle. This playful mental shift reduces stress and encourages resilience. It trains your brain to respond to challenges with lightness rather than heaviness.

Engaging with others who appreciate humor also strengthens your daily habit. Surrounding yourself with people who laugh easily and share your comedic style provides a supportive environment for humor to flourish.

Group laughter has a contagious effect, amplifying joy and social bonding.

Importantly, cultivating humor as a daily habit requires intentionality and patience. Like any skill, it improves with practice. Some days will feel easier than others, but maintaining a lighthearted attitude over time enhances your ability to find humor in a variety of situations.

Humor as a daily habit contributes to better health. Regular laughter lowers stress hormones, boosts immune function, and improves mood. By making humor a priority, you invest in your physical and emotional well-being.

Humor is a powerful, accessible habit that can transform everyday life. Through awareness, routine, social connection, and playful mindset shifts, you can cultivate humor daily—inviting more laughter, resilience, and joy into your world. Embracing humor as a habit unlocks laughter's hidden power, enriching every moment.

Laughter is a natural, spontaneous expression—but in today's busy, stressful world, it often takes a backseat to responsibilities, worries, and routine. Cultivating laughter intentionally can transform our daily experience, boosting well-being, strengthening relation-ships, and enriching life's meaning. This chapter offers practical strategies and mindset shifts to invite more laughter into everyday life, making it a habit rather than a rare delight.

The first step to cultivating laughter is recognizing its value and making space for it. This means prioritizing joy as an essential part of self-care and mental health, rather than seeing laughter as frivolous or unproductive. Setting an intention to seek humor daily can shift our perspective, opening eyes to the small moments of amusement and delight around us—from funny conversations to playful interactions or unexpected surprises.

Building a humorous mindset helps too. This involves developing the ability to find lightness even in difficult situations, to laugh at our own imperfections, and to embrace a playful curiosity about life. Practicing self-compassion and letting go of rigid seriousness create fertile ground for humor. Techniques such as reframing challenges with humor, storytelling, or playful exaggeration can help transform stress into laughter.

Social connection is a powerful laughter catalyst. Spending time with people who have a good sense of humor, sharing funny stories, watching comedies together, or engaging in playful activities naturally sparks laughter. Being around positive, lighthearted individuals can raise our own laughter frequency and mood. Conversely, surrounding ourselves with negativity or stressors tends to dampen humor.

Intentional laughter exercises are another effective tool. Laughter yoga, guided laughter sessions, or even laughing at oneself on purpose activate the body's laughter response, triggering the health and emotional benefits even without a comedic stimulus. These practices demonstrate that laughter can be a choice and a skill, not just a spontaneous reaction.

Technology offers creative ways to access humor daily. Listening to comedy podcasts, watching funny videos, or following humor-focused social media channels can provide a quick laughter boost. However, mindful use is important—too much screen time or negative online content can undermine well-being.

Creating an environment that encourages laughter also matters. This might mean decorating spaces with humorous art, keeping joke books handy, or setting up "laughter breaks" at work or home. Encouraging children to engage in playful humor nurtures their social and emotional development and models lifelong laughter habits.

Finally, patience and persistence are key. Cultivating laughter is a practice that deepens over time. Some days will be easier than others, but even small moments of laughter accumulate, improving mood and resilience. Being open to humor in its many forms—from silly to clever, from quiet chuckles to full belly laughs—broadens our capacity to enjoy life's lighthearted side.

In conclusion, cultivating laughter daily enriches our health, relationships, and emotional well-being. With intentionality, openness, and practice, laughter can become a reliable resource and joyful habit that brightens everyday life. By welcoming more laughter, we invite greater happiness, connection, and resilience into our world.

Chapter 21: Stories of Humor in Daily Life

Humor thrives in the everyday moments that often go unnoticed—the little surprises, quirky mishaps, and spontaneous interactions that sprinkle our lives with laughter. In this chapter, we explore real-life stories that showcase how humor naturally unfolds in daily life, reminding us that laughter is always within reach, even amid routine or challenges.

One memorable story comes from a busy office where a misplaced memo sparked an unintended comedy. A manager accidentally sent an email meant for a small team to the entire company, filled with playful critiques and inside jokes. Instead of embarrassment, the message became a source of laughter and connection, breaking down formal barriers and creating a more relaxed, friendly atmosphere. This incident highlights how humor can emerge from mistakes and lighten workplace stress.

At home, a parent shares a tale of bedtime chaos turned comedic gold. Their toddler, adamant about choosing their own pajamas, ended up wearing mismatched socks, a superhero cape, and a bathrobe as a "dress." The parent's initial frustration melted into laughter as they snapped a photo and joined the child's imaginative play. This story illustrates how embracing humor in parenting strengthens bonds and turns everyday struggles into joyful memories.

In a more public setting, a commuter recalls a crowded subway ride interrupted by a street performer's witty antics. The performer engaged passengers with clever jokes, playful mimicry, and lighthearted challenges. The shared laughter among strangers created a momentary community, easing the stress of rush hour and reminding everyone of their shared humanity. This experience shows how humor can unite people, even fleetingly, in unlikely places.

Another story involves a retiree who found humor as a tool for resilience after losing a beloved pet. Instead of dwelling solely on grief, they began writing lighthearted anecdotes about the pet's mischievous behavior and quirks, sharing these stories with friends and online communities. The laughter that followed became a balm for sorrow and a way to honor cherished memories, demonstrating humor's healing power.

In friendships, a group of lifelong pals recounts how their annual game night is peppered with hilarious inside jokes and playful teasing. These shared humorous rituals have woven a rich tapestry of connection and joy over decades, showing how humor nurtures lasting relationships and creates treasured traditions.

These stories reveal common themes: humor often arises spontaneously, frequently from imperfections or unexpected moments. It connects people across ages, cultures, and circumstances. Most importantly, it reminds us that laughter is a natural, accessible response to life's complexities.

By reflecting on these stories, readers can recognize opportunities for humor in their own lives. Whether in work, family, public spaces, or personal challenges, humor invites lightness and connection. It's a daily treasure that transforms ordinary moments into joyful experiences.

In conclusion, everyday stories of humor illustrate laughter's hidden power to uplift, heal, and unite. Embracing these moments with openness and playfulness allows us to cultivate a life rich in joy and resilience—proof that humor is always just around the corner.

Chapter 22: Humorous Anecdotes

Humor often shines brightest in the small, unexpected moments that catch us off guard and remind us not to take life too seriously. This chapter shares a collection of lighthearted anecdotes that capture laughter's spontaneous magic, illustrating how humor enriches everyday life and reveals laughter's hidden power.

The Case of the Disappearing Keys

One morning, a woman spent nearly an hour searching frantically for her car keys before realizing she'd been holding them the whole time—in her hand. The moment she discovered this, she couldn't help but laugh at herself. This simple mistake became a running joke in her family, a reminder that sometimes the answers we seek are right in front of us, waiting for a laugh to break the tension.

The Cooking Catastrophe

A man decided to impress his date by cooking a fancy dinner. Confidently, he followed the recipe but somehow set off the fire alarm—not once, but twice. Between frantic attempts to open windows and fan the smoke away, he and his date burst into uncontrollable laughter. The charred meal was a disaster, but the humor and shared experience made the evening unforgettable.

The Elevator

In a crowded elevator, someone pressed every floor button "just for fun," causing a slow, stop-and-go ride that left passengers exchanging amused glances. One quick-witted passenger joked, "Looks like we're taking the scenic route!" The elevator filled with laughter, turning an annoyance into a moment of camaraderie.

The Misheard Text

A teenager meant to text their mom, "I'm on my way," but autocorrect changed it to, "I'm on my whale." The mom responded with a whale emoji, and the two enjoyed a playful texting exchange filled with puns and laughter that lightened the usual rush to get home.

The Dog's New Trick

A woman's dog learned to "speak" on command—barking in a series of hilarious tones. One day, the dog barked so convincingly during a video call that coworkers paused, wondering if a colleague had suddenly brought their pet to work. The laughter that followed eased the tension of a long meeting and sparked ongoing jokes about the "talking dog."

The Wardrobe Malfunction

A man rushed out the door for an important meeting, only to realize halfway there that he was wearing mismatched shoes—one black dress shoe, one sneaker. Instead of panic, he laughed and embraced the "fashion statement," which sparked conversations and connections throughout the day.

The Surprise Zoom Background

During a serious virtual meeting, a colleague's toddler wandered into the room, wearing a superhero cape and holding a toy sword. The unexpected "guest star" stole the show, causing everyone to laugh and momentarily forget their work stress.

These anecdotes show how humor naturally appears in everyday life's quirks, mistakes, and surprises. They remind us that laughter often requires only openness to the moment and a willingness to see the lighter side.

Incorporating such stories into your life—and sharing your own—can create joy, reduce stress, and deepen connections. They exemplify how humor's hidden power thrives in the ordinary, waiting to be discovered and celebrated.

Chapter 23: Classic Funny Jokes

Humor has taken many forms throughout the ages—satire, slapstick, irony, and wordplay to name just a few. But few things have stood the test of time quite like a good, classic joke. The kind that gets a smile even when you've heard it before. The kind that children love to repeat and adults can't help but chuckle at. These jokes aren't built on shock or sarcasm, but on simplicity, timing, and a universal sense of fun. This chapter is a celebration of classic funny jokes—the timeless treasures that keep laughter alive across generations.

Why did the chicken cross the road?
To get to the other side!
It's the joke everyone knows—and groans at—but it's also a perfect example of anti-humor, where the punchline defies expectations by being absurdly obvious. The charm lies in its simplicity.

Knock knock.

Who's there?
Boo.
Boo who?
Don't cry, it's just a joke!
Knock-knock jokes are a staple of childhood humor, and for good reason. They teach timing, structure, and how to set up a punchline—all while being endlessly adaptable.

I told my wife she was drawing her eyebrows too high.
She looked surprised.
This clever bit of wordplay works because it turns a visual expression into a double meaning. It's punny, snappy, and instantly funny.

Why don't scientists trust atoms?
Because they make up everything!
Science jokes like this blend curiosity with comedy. It's educational and silly at the same time—a formula that works in every setting.

Why did the scarecrow win an award?
Because he was outstanding in his field.
This groaner is beloved precisely because it's a pun so

obvious that it's brilliant. It invites a smile and a small shake of the head—the classic "dad joke" reaction.

What do you call fake spaghetti?
An impasta!
Food puns have always been crowd-pleasers. They're easy to remember, quick to tell, and work in nearly any audience.

How does a penguin build its house?
Igloos it together.
Animal jokes are universally loved, especially when they include wordplay like this. They're often used in children's books and classrooms because of their warmth and accessibility.

I asked the librarian if the library had books on paranoia.
She whispered, "They're right behind you."
This joke has a mini story built into it, complete with tension and payoff. It also plays on the setting, making it relatable and unexpected.

Did you hear about the claustrophobic astronaut?
He needed a little space.

Another example of modern wordplay, this joke takes a relatable human feeling and matches it with a humorous twist.

I used to play piano by ear.
Now I use my hands.
Classic one-liners like this harken back to the golden age of comedy clubs and vaudeville acts. They rely on misdirection and clever phrasing to land their laughs.

What makes these jokes so enduring isn't just that they're funny—it's that they're *friendly*. They don't rely on putting others down or crossing lines. They're inclusive, clean, and quick. In a world that sometimes seems overly complicated, a classic joke is a refreshing reminder that joy can be simple.

These timeless gems often serve as an entry point into humor. Children use them to learn how jokes work. Adults use them to lighten tense situations. Grandparents use them to connect with younger generations. Their reach is universal, and their value immense.

Whether you're in a waiting room, at the dinner table, on a long car ride, or cheering up a friend, a well-timed classic joke can do wonders. It brings a break in the routine, a shared laugh, and a moment of pure human connection. And that's exactly what laughter is about—

building bridges, lifting moods, and adding a little light to our lives.

So, the next time someone says, "Tell me a joke," don't underestimate the power of the classics. They've survived for a reason. And who knows? You might just be the reason someone smiles today.

Chapter 24: When Not to Laugh

Laughter is a beautiful and powerful human expression. It can bring joy, break tension, connect people, and even heal emotional wounds. But like all powerful tools, laughter must be used with care. There are moments when laughter, even if unintentional, can hurt rather than heal—times when silence, empathy, or solemnity are the more appropriate responses. Understanding when *not* to laugh is as important as knowing how to find humor in everyday life.

One of the most obvious moments when laughter should be restrained is during grief. In the presence of someone who is mourning, laughter can seem callous or disrespectful, especially if it appears out of place or inattentive to their pain. While there are certainly times when shared stories or memories can bring a bittersweet smile, those moments must be approached with sensitivity. The laughter that naturally arises from remembering a loved one's quirks or joyful times can be a balm, but forced or misplaced humor can alienate and wound.

Similarly, moments of personal confession or vulnerability are rarely appropriate for laughter. When someone is opening up about trauma, failure, insecurity, or fear, laughter—particularly if it sounds dismissive—can shut them down emotionally. Even if their story includes humorous elements, your first response should be empathy and presence. Save the chuckle for later, if they invite it.

Laughter should also be carefully monitored in professional or formal settings. Making a joke during a serious meeting, a courtroom proceeding, or a solemn ceremony can come across as immature or disrespectful. Humor can be a valuable communication tool, but timing and context are everything. A well-timed light comment can diffuse tension, while an ill-timed laugh can derail trust and credibility.

It's important, too, to be conscious of laughter that excludes, mocks, or targets others. Laughing at someone rather than with them is one of the most harmful misuses of humor. Sarcasm, ridicule, and derisive laughter can scar deeply, especially when aimed at someone who is already feeling insecure or marginalized. It might feel harmless in the moment, especially among friends or peers, but the ripple effects of this kind of laughter can linger long after the moment has passed.

Even in entertainment, not all laughter is harmless. Comedians and performers walk a fine line between edgy and offensive. When humor relies on stereotypes, shaming, or punching down, it's worth questioning its value. A laugh that comes at the expense of someone's dignity, identity, or culture may entertain one group while deeply offending another. Social awareness and empathy should guide not only how we laugh, but also what we choose to laugh at.

There are also cultural differences to consider. In some countries or social settings, laughing too loudly, too frequently, or at certain topics can be viewed as disrespectful or inappropriate. What may be funny and lighthearted in one context may be taboo or rude in another. Being aware of your surroundings and adapting your behavior to respect the setting is part of the emotional intelligence that comes with mature laughter.

Finally, laughter should never be used as a mask to avoid difficult emotions. Sometimes we laugh when we're nervous, embarrassed, or afraid. While this kind of nervous laughter is involuntary and very human, it can prevent genuine emotional expression. Constantly laughing off pain or discomfort can keep us from processing what we truly feel. It's okay not to be okay—and it's okay not to laugh.

Knowing when not to laugh doesn't mean becoming somber or overly serious. Rather, it means becoming more attuned to others, more thoughtful with our responses, and more respectful of the emotional realities people carry. Laughter, at its best, is inclusive, uplifting, and timely. Like music, it's not just about the notes—it's about the pauses in between. And in those pauses, we often find deeper connection, understanding, and grace.

Chapter 25: Living a Life That Laughs

To live a life that laughs is to embrace joy, resilience, and connection as daily companions. It's not about chasing constant happiness or ignoring life's hardships; rather, it's about cultivating a mindset and lifestyle that welcome humor and laughter as essential elements of well-being and fulfillment. This chapter explores what it means to live a life infused with laughter and how you can invite more of this enriching energy into your everyday existence.

Living a life that laughs begins with intention. It requires a conscious choice to prioritize lightness and play, even amid challenges. This doesn't mean dismissing serious moments or avoiding difficult emotions; instead, it means allowing humor to coexist with complexity, providing relief and perspective. By nurturing laughter as a practice, you build emotional flexibility and a more joyful outlook.

One of the hallmarks of a life that laughs is the ability to find humor in the ordinary. Everyday experiences, from commuting to conversations, become opportunities for amusement and delight. This perspective transforms routine into a playground for joy, making life feel lighter and more vibrant. Developing this mindset takes mindfulness—paying attention to moments that spark a smile or chuckle and savoring them fully.

Relationships flourish when laughter is present. Sharing humor with friends, family, and colleagues creates bonds that withstand stress and deepen intimacy. A life that laughs is often a life rich in connection, where people feel seen, accepted, and joyful together. Humor becomes a language of love and understanding, breaking down walls and inviting warmth.

Resilience is another vital benefit of living a life that laughs. Laughter acts as a buffer against adversity, reducing the impact of stress and helping you bounce back more quickly from setbacks. Those who cultivate humor tend to approach problems with creativity and openness, viewing challenges as temporary and manageable rather than overwhelming.

Practically, living a life that laughs involves creating habits and environments that support humor. Surround yourself with playful people, seek out comedy and joyful experiences, and don't hesitate to be silly or lighthearted yourself. Incorporate humor into your daily routines— whether through jokes, funny media, or playful rituals— to keep laughter flowing consistently.

Importantly, living a life that laughs also means embracing imperfections and mistakes with kindness.

When you can laugh at your own foibles and see the humor in mishaps, you release the grip of perfectionism and invite freedom. This compassionate humor fosters self-acceptance and eases inner tension.

Ultimately, a life that laughs is a life lived fully—present, engaged, and open to joy. It honors the healing and connecting power of laughter as a vital thread woven through the fabric of everyday living. By choosing to live this way, you not only enrich your own experience but also inspire others to embrace humor and happiness alongside you.

In the next chapter, we will explore practical ways to nurture and sustain this joyful way of living. For now, reflect on what it means to you personally to live a life that laughs—and how you might begin inviting more laughter into your world today.

Chapter 26: How to Nurture Laughter

Laughter, like any positive habit, can be cultivated with care and intention. While many wait for laughter to strike like lightning, the truth is that it can be gently nurtured into daily life. Creating a life filled with laughter begins with small shifts in perspective, simple actions, and an openness to finding humor in unexpected places. This chapter explores practical, everyday approaches to weaving more laughter into your life.

One of the simplest ways to invite more laughter into your day is by starting with a smile. A smile, though small, carries significant emotional weight. It sends a signal to your brain that you are safe, content, and open to connection. Smiling in the mirror each morning may feel awkward at first, but it sets a positive tone and paves the way for spontaneous laughter. Smiles are also contagious. Offering one to a stranger, a co-worker, or a family member can create an unexpected ripple of goodwill and even lead to a shared chuckle.

Your environment plays a major role in influencing your mood and your capacity to laugh. Creating a laughter-friendly space can be as simple as pinning a funny comic on the fridge, displaying photos from joyful moments, or keeping a playlist of your favorite comedy clips handy. When your surroundings reflect a sense of playfulness and joy, they can act as daily reminders not to take life too seriously. Choosing to be surrounded by people who uplift you with their humor and positivity is equally important. Laughter thrives in community, and time spent with lighthearted individuals helps cultivate your own sense of humor.

Laughter doesn't always need to be spontaneous—it can be scheduled. Taking a laughter break during the day can be as rejuvenating as a power nap or a walk in nature. Watching a short comedy sketch, listening to a humorous podcast, or reading something amusing during a lunch break can reset your mood and bring fresh energy into the rest of your day. When laughter becomes a regular practice instead of a rare occurrence, it has a cumulative effect on well-being.

There is also great power in laughing with others. Shared laughter builds bonds, dissolves tension, and fosters trust. It's important to laugh *with* others, never *at* their expense. Invite playfulness into your conversations, enjoy games that spark silliness, and share stories that highlight life's absurd moments. Being open to laughter in social settings often means being willing to be a little vulnerable or self-deprecating, which in turn can make others feel more at ease.

Another powerful method to nurture laughter is to practice it—even when there's nothing funny happening. This might sound unusual, but methods like laughter yoga are built on this idea. Begin by producing a gentle laugh on purpose. It might feel forced, but with a bit of persistence, the laughter often becomes genuine. The body doesn't fully distinguish between spontaneous and voluntary laughter; in both cases, it reaps the same physiological and psychological rewards. Over time, this practice can train your mind to find joy more easily and reduce the weight of daily stress.

Keeping a humor journal is another effective way to increase your awareness of laughter in daily life. At the end of each day, jot down a moment that made you smile or laugh, a joke you heard, or something amusing that you noticed. This small act of reflection reinforces a mindset that seeks out joy. Over time, your journal becomes a personal collection of light-hearted memories that you can revisit during harder days, serving as a reminder of your ability to experience and create joy.

Laughter can also be a tool for reframing negative situations. While some experiences are too serious for humor, many day-to-day frustrations can be softened with a lighter perspective. If you spill coffee on your shirt before a meeting or lock your keys in your car, try to view the situation through a comedic lens. Finding the absurdity in these moments helps release tension and promotes emotional resilience. Cultivating this response takes practice, but it can turn potential irritations into personal anecdotes you'll laugh about later.

A playful spirit is often the missing piece for many adults who take life—and themselves—a bit too seriously. Reconnecting with your sense of play can unlock laughter naturally. Whether you're making silly faces at a baby, dancing while doing chores, talking to your pet in a funny voice, or creating an impromptu story, the freedom to be playful invites joy into your day. It's a reminder that laughter doesn't require an audience or a punchline—just a willingness to engage with life a little more loosely.

Consuming media that brings you joy is a deliberate choice that supports laughter. In a world full of serious news and constant alerts, it's easy to get pulled into stress and worry. Balance your information intake with light-hearted content—books, movies, shows, or online videos that genuinely make you laugh. Seek out storytellers and comedians who match your sense of humor. These simple sources of amusement can help you relax and keep your emotional balance in check.

Lastly, consider joining a laughter group or club. These groups, both in-person and virtual, focus on shared laughter through playful exercises, stories, and community. Even if you're shy or hesitant at first, the experience of laughing together with others—without any pressure to perform—can be deeply healing and surprisingly fun.

In the end, nurturing laughter isn't about always being funny or ignoring life's difficulties. It's about choosing joy where you can, sharing lightness with others, and giving yourself permission to laugh often and without guilt. Laughter is not just a pleasant reaction; it's a powerful, practical tool for health, connection, and personal transformation. When you water the seeds of laughter daily, your life will blossom with more happiness, resilience, and heart.

Chapter 27: The Future of Laughter

As we look toward the future, laughter's hidden power is poised to play an even more vital role in our rapidly changing world. Advances in science, technology, and social understanding are opening new avenues to harness laughter's benefits for health, education, work, and community. This chapter explores emerging trends, innovations, and challenges that will shape how laughter is valued and cultivated in the years ahead.

Scientific research continues to uncover the biological and psychological mechanisms behind laughter, deepening our understanding of its healing potential. Cutting-edge studies in neuroscience and psychology are exploring how laughter influences brain plasticity, immune function, and emotional regulation. These insights pave the way for new therapeutic approaches that integrate laughter into treatments for mental illness, chronic pain, neurodegenerative diseases, and more.

Technology is expanding laughter's reach and accessibility. Virtual reality (VR) and augmented reality (AR) offer immersive environments where people can experience shared humor regardless of geographic distance. AI-powered companions and humor bots are emerging, designed to deliver personalized jokes and laughter prompts to improve mood and combat loneliness. Online communities centered around humor continue to grow, connecting people worldwide through shared laughter.

In education, laughter will likely become an even more intentional part of curricula and learning environments. As educators recognize humor's role in fostering creativity, engagement, and mental health, laughter-based interventions may be integrated systematically from early childhood through adult education. Digital tools that incorporate gamified humor could revolutionize how knowledge is conveyed and retained.

Workplaces are also evolving to prioritize well-being, with laughter playing a key role. Forward-thinking organizations will adopt laughter-centric wellness programs, incorporating humor coaching, laughter breaks, and social activities to boost morale, creativity, and teamwork. Remote and hybrid work models will leverage virtual humor to maintain connection and reduce isolation among distributed teams.

Socially, laughter can be a force for inclusion and empathy in a world marked by division and stress. Humor that bridges cultural gaps and challenges prejudice may help foster greater understanding and solidarity. However, ethical considerations about the use and misuse of humor—such as avoiding harmful stereotypes or exclusion—will require ongoing attention.

Challenges remain, such as overcoming societal tendencies to undervalue play and laughter in adult life, and ensuring that laughter-based interventions are inclusive and culturally sensitive. But the growing recognition of laughter's multifaceted power is a hopeful sign that laughter will be embraced as a fundamental human need.

Ultimately, the future of laughter is intertwined with humanity's pursuit of health, connection, and meaning. By continuing to explore and celebrate laughter's hidden power, we can build a world where joy and resilience flourish amid life's challenges.

Chapter 28: Embracing Laughter's Power

As we reach the conclusion of this exploration into laughter's hidden power, it becomes clear that laughter is much more than a simple reaction or momentary escape—it is a profound force that enriches our health, relationships, and resilience. Throughout this book, we have uncovered how laughter connects us to our humanity, unlocks well-being, and fosters joy even in the face of life's challenges.

Laughter is a universal language that transcends age, culture, and circumstance. It breaks down barriers, creates bonds, and invites empathy. Whether it's a shared joke between friends, a lighthearted moment in a stressful day, or the ability to laugh at ourselves, laughter has the remarkable ability to lift spirits and nurture connection.

Science confirms what ancient wisdom long knew: laughter boosts physical health by reducing stress hormones, strengthening the immune system, and promoting cardiovascular wellness. It enhances mental health by elevating mood, releasing endorphins, and improving emotional resilience. These benefits remind us that laughter is not just pleasant—it is vital.

Moreover, laughter is a skill and a habit that can be cultivated. By finding our funny bone, learning to laugh at ourselves, and integrating humor into daily life, we empower ourselves to invite more joy and lightness. We have seen how humor can transform workplaces, classrooms, and communities, creating environments where creativity and collaboration flourish.

The stories and anecdotes shared throughout this book demonstrate laughter's spontaneity and accessibility. Humor is always near, hidden in the small moments of imperfection, surprise, and human connection. Recognizing and embracing these moments allows us to tap into laughter's power whenever we choose.

As you close this book, consider laughter not as an occasional delight but as a vital practice—one that nurtures health, deepens relationships, and enriches your life's meaning. Invite laughter intentionally, share it generously, and let it be a source of strength and joy through all seasons.

In a world often marked by stress and uncertainty, laughter stands as a beacon of light and hope. Its hidden power is yours to discover and wield. May you carry this gift forward, spreading joy and resilience wherever you go.

Thank you for joining this journey into laughter's transformative magic. Keep laughing, keep connecting, and let the hidden power of laughter illuminate your path.

ABOUT THE AUTHOR

Joe R. Eagleman (1936-) was born on a farm near West Plains Missouri. He received the PhD from the University of Missouri in 1963 and was a professor at the University of Kansas for 39 years. He taught thousands of students about Atmospheric Science through his courses there and many thousands more

 through four different textbooks used by over a hundred universities over a span of several decades. He directed a successful experiment on Skylab, funded by NASA, and invented a tornado in his laboratory that was used by Universal Studios for a 50 ft. tornado attraction in the Twister Building in Orlando Florida for several decades. It can still be seen at the Exploratorium in San Francisco.

He is the author of a technical book on severe thunderstorms that includes his tornado safety research

which resulted in changes that were adopted nationally. His autobiography, *Name Your Price*, tells of his early life on a farm where he was the 11th of 12 children. It includes his work as a scientist as well as a number of unusual hobbies including those as an artist, musician, luthier, marksman, taxidermist, world traveler and other endeavors.

He has also published his second autobiography, *Monumental Moments*, that captures the most significant times of his life and *Eagleman Stories* that contains stories from his life as well as his 11 siblings and his parents.

Since his retirement he has published numerous books and recorded four albums of original music. For more information see http://www.JoeEagleman.com.